• RACING •

FROM THE EARLY YEARS OF PUNCH

• RACING •

*It's enough to make
a horse laugh*

Special Edition for PAST TIMES® Oxford, England

First published in Great Britain by
Constable & Robinson Ltd
3 The Lanchesters
162 Fulham Palace Rd
London W6 9ER

This edition published by arrangement with Punch Ltd.
Copyright © Punch Limited 2000

All rights reserved. No part of this publication
may be reproduced, stored in a retrieval system,
or transmitted in any form or by any means,
electronic, mechanical, photocopying, recording
or otherwise, without the prior permission of
the copyright owner.

A CIP catalogue record of this book is available
from the British Library

ISBN 1-84119-198-1

Design and typeset by Tony and Penny Mills
Printed and bound in the EC

The publishers have made every effort to trace
copyright holders for pictures and text in this
book, but they beg forgiveness of any who
have been overlooked. They will be happy
to rectify this in any future editions.

PAST TIMES®

• CONTENTS •

• OVER THE •
STICKS

AINTREE

THERE are many famous courses
   In the width of English ground
Where the steeple-chasing horses
   And the rainbow silks go round:
But it's Aintree, Aintree, Aintree
   Where the champion 'chasers run,
Where there's courage to be tested
   And there's glory to be won.

There the dancing sunbeams quiver
    On the colours as they glide,
Or the mists of Mersey river
    Give but glimpses of the ride;
But it's always Aintree – Aintree
    Where the pride of England waits
To hear the turf responding
    To the drum of racing-plates.

Maurice Hall

'I want something that won't shrink in the water-jump.'

THE GRAND NATIONAL

The horse that concluded it must be the proper thing to do.

'The BBC declined to elaborate on the means by which the description would be given, but said they would "not necessarily" send their own observers.' – *Daily Telegraph*

There the gallant lads are weighing
 For the ride they love so well;
There the serried crowds are swaying
 As they hear the saddling-bell.
And it's Aintree, Aintree, Aintree,
 Boot and saddle, fence and fall,
And it calls to sporting England
 As no other course can call.

W.H.O.

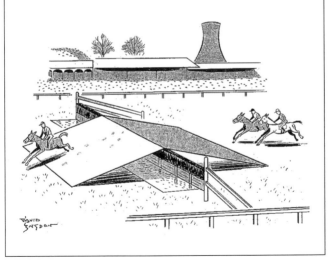

A STEEPLE-CHASE RIDER'S DIARY
[1901]

Tuesday. Due at Mudbury Steeplechases. Am riding in two races there.

Wednesday: In first race of yesterday horse ran against post; hurt knee-cap, lost whip, broke stirrup-leather, but finally won by a length. Not so lucky in next race. Was leading, when horse blundered, smashed guard-rail and turned tail over head into next field. Sprained wrist, broke bridge of nose, and was rather badly shaken. However, nothing to really hurt. Have to get down into Thrustershire tonight, as I am to ride in three races there tomorrow.

Thursday: Got second in opening race, after being 'cannoned' over last fence, and my mount knocked on to his knees and nose. Bad luck in next race, as riderless horse galloped right across my mount just as he 'took off' at biggest fence on the course. Four other horses jumped on, or over, me. Nett result, two ribs fractured, silk jacket cut off my back, and little finger smashed. Annoying, this, as am unable to ride in last race of afternoon.

Friday: Hurrah! Found very smart doctor, who has

patched me up splendidly and bandaged ribs so well that I can hardly breathe. Shall ride in Grand Annual today, and think, with a bit of luck, that I shall win.

A week later. Where am I? Ah, I see – in bed. How long is it since–? Oh, a week; is it really? And what's happened, what have I–? Oh, concussion of brain, collar-bone and right arm broken and some ribs dislocated – is that all? Very vexing that, whilst I have been insensible, the Grand

OUR AMATEUR STEEPLECHASE MEETING
'They're OFF!'

THE SUBSTITUTE

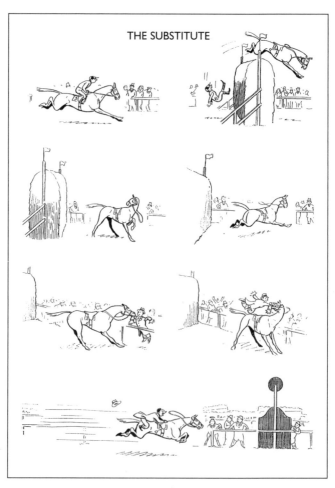

COUNTRY RACES

Gentlemen riders, who are so like professional jocks, you can hardly tell the difference!

National has been run. Where did my horse finish in it? Oh, broke his neck, eh? H'm, that's bad luck. And his jockey? Oh, still unconscious, eh? Wonder how long it will be before I can get out, as I must be doctored up in time to ride *The Smasher* in the Great Kilham and Krushem Stakes, next month.

· A WAITING ·
GAME

from
REAL SPORT AT RACES
[1869]

HAVE you not often wondered at the interest which people generally take in races, insomuch as seriously to care about seeing them for their own sake? For the sake of a holiday and eating and drinking, that is another affair. That of course we understand: but in merely witnessing a lot of horses gallop, what is there more than anybody but an ass can perfectly well imagine? At Goodwood however, the other day I imagine you would have been rather amused by an incident which a contemporary thus describes, and speaks of as though really considering it an untoward one:

In the Bentinck Memorial stakes the only horse found to dispute the pretensions of the famous and beautiful *Formosa* was *Blueskin*, who had already run a punishing

'They "also run" who only stand and wait.'

long race with *Restitution*. *Blueskin's* jockey consequently had orders to ride a waiting race. But *Formosa's* jockey had received similar orders, because the mare's force is speed, and not lasting qualities. When they were started, therefore, each jockey immediately tried to wait behind the other, and their respective animals soon dropped down to a canter, then into a walk, and finally to the astonishment of the beholders, actually stopped and stood facing each other for a quarter of an hour. Never before had such a sight been witnessed on a race-course, and it is to be hoped, never will again.

Now that is what I call sport.

• ON THE •
FLAT

from
WHY THEY GO TO ASCOT
[1876]

Lady Upperton's reasons. Because it is really quite the thing to do. Because sweet Angelina will be sure to meet dear Lord Edwin there. Because a judicious lunch often leads to a good proposal. Because the girls have set their hearts upon it, and have ordered their dresses.

Mrs. Redpaynt Flirtington's reasons. Because business of importance will keep Mr. R. Flirtington in Town. Because she is sure to be amused. Because the children at home are such a bother. Because in her new dress she will look six-and-thirty.

Mr. Samuel Shoddy of New York's reason. Because he may as well take Ascot on his way to St. Petersburg, via Paris, Vienna, Malta, Rome, and Constantinople.

Mr. Romeo Montague's reason. Because she is to be there.

MANNERS AND MODES AT ASCOT

Although the younger racing set undoubtedly contributes to the picturesqueness of the scene –

it is the leaven of die-hards that gives to the Royal meeting its unique *cachet.*

Miss Juliet Capulet's reason. Because *he* said he was going!

Le Marquis Chateau de Pommes-Frite's reason. Because he is a thorough 'gentlemans-ridère' and loves the 'high-life' English.

The Duchess of Brompton's reasons. Because it's an agreeable change after the dusty Park, and the over-heated ball-room. Because lunch on the lawn is rather pleasant, than otherwise. Because one way of spending one's time is about as good as another way.

The Duke of Brompton's reasons. Because the Duchess wishes it.

Lord and Lady Mudgold's (new creation) reason. Because the dear Duke and the sweet Duchess are *sure* to be there.

Mr. and Mrs. Plantagenet de Snuké's (née Snooks) reason. Because the STUART DE JOYNES (who ten years ago were called JONES) will have an opportunity of seeing LORD AND LADY MUDGOLD return our bows.

Mr. Punch's reasons. Because it is my pleasure to pick up good characters.

Policeman's reasons. Because it's my duty to lock up bad ones.

THE BULLYON-BOUNDERMERES AT ASCOT.

Mrs B-B. 'I despair of you, Joseph. *Think* of you refusing to back the Duke's horse , and telling the dear duchess that you had put your money on a horrid outsider owned by another outsider.'

Mr B-B. 'Sorry, my dear. Bur I 'ad a tip from a pal in the know, and, after all, I won my money.'

Mrs B-B. 'That's no use. You'd have better lost in good company.'

MANNERS AND MODES AT ASCOT

Reefing topsails in breezy weather.

ASCOT, AND SO ON
[1930]

All the dresses in the leafy garden
    Were long as long could be,
Lovely as the dress of the late Dolly Varden,
    Filmy as the foam of the sea,
And the plaints and the sobs of the short-dress lovers
    Faded on the breeze and died,
For the legs of the ladies were covered by covers
    Impeding their stride.

None of the dresses in the Royal Enclosure
    (If anybody cares two pins)
Yielded the least little trace of exposure
    To any one's shins;
Souls that were swept by rapture or passion,
    Dowagers, débutantes, flirts,
Followed the dictates of present-day fashion
    Regarding their skirts.

All of the gentlemen were wearing trousers,
    At least so far as I know,
Earls, Ambassadors, and sandwich-browsers,
    Simpkins and Johnnie Doe;

Legs that were mighty or lowly in their places
    Each had the pantaloon
Reaching from the coy concealment of the braces
    Down to the shoon.

None of them, Duke or philosopher or farmer
    Strutted in thigh-high boots;
Still less did any of them put on armour
    Over their morning-suits;
And the trees of a Berkshire June were apparelled
    (Or so I am given to understand)
In the green they have always worn since Harold
    Was lord of this land.

Fashion and history! Mutable forces!
    Nature alarmingly crude!
Strange is the world; I must note that the horses
    Were pretty well nude;
Times are gone by when, liking it or loathing,
    Under the tournament's box
Gentlemen's quadrupeds had to wear clothing
    As far as the hocks.

Petticoats, hose, galligaskins and waders,
    Trousers, Court breeches and greaves,

Crinolines, woad, chain-mail for Crusaders,
    Lingerie, laces and leaves!
This thing is old and that thing is recent,
    This thing is short and that high,
Some legs are shameful and some legs are decent –
    And who can say why?

EVOE

'My dear, wait till you see my new colours – sapphire jacket with
peach sleeves, cerise hoops and a midnight blue cap.'

POEM ON THE DERBY
[1932]

Now sing me of horses
  Renowned for their breed,
Exerting their forces
  With promptness and speed:
The lark's in the heavens,
  My brolly is furled,
The favourite's at sevens,
  All's right with the world.

I say. old fellow. how do you go to the Derby
this year?

Oh. the old way—
hamper and four.

1853

A GOODWOOD MEETING
[1908]

Do you forget that Goodwood Day
  And all the vows we vowed,
As we together strolled away
  Far from the madding crowd?
How wistfully you shook your head
  As, when our fingers met
In one last lingering clasp, I said,
  'Will you forget?'

Do you forget the dream you had
  About a number up,
That haunted you, and made you mad
  To plunge upon the Cup?
And though I swore dreams always lied,
  And warned you not to bet,
'A pony on for me,' you cried,
  'And *don't* forget!'

I put that pony on for you,
    Though much against my will;
The dream, of course, did not come true,
    And I am wondering still
If you regard the vows you made
    As lightly as your debt;
For I begin to be afraid
    You *do* forget.

Afternoon tea at Ascot. Pooling our losses.

· SOCIETY · AT THE RACES

'A FRIEND'
[1911]

I MET Reginald by chance in Jermyn Street and, accepting the invitation which he omitted to offer me, accompanied him up to his rooms.

I was soon to regret my good nature, however, for Reginald was in a state of the deepest dejection.

'Reginald,' I said – in lighter mood I call him Reggie, but I saw at once that this was not a Reggie day – 'Reginald, you are off colour: What is the nature of your trouble? Financial, physical, or social?'

I know Reginald's worldly ambitions and was not surprised therefore that at the last word he winced painfully, and pointed to a pile of weekly illustrated papers.

I snatched them up one after the other, and hastily scanned their pages, fearing I knew not what.

'I can't find anything,' I said at length, 'unless it's

THE ADAPTABLE SEX
Picture of society couple who, engaged in a furious quarrel are
snapped by a press photographer.

these portraits of you at various race-meetings. I don't say you look extraordinarily handsome in any –' But he cut me short.

'Don't you see, you ass?' he said. Read the writing "The Hon. Craven Coward in the Enclosure *with a friend*!" "General Waitingroom *talking with a friend*!" "Sir Tiddley and Lady Winks *and a friend*." That's what makes me so wild. Why must I always be "a friend"? Why can't they say who I am? Aren't I as good as the Winkses? Or old Waitingroom? But I've got them this time,' he went on, cooling down a little 'When I was at Goodwood I managed to get taken *absolutely alone*.'

AN EVEN BREAK

A turf correspondent hopes that there will be no more horse doping this season. Flat-racing *must* be on the level.

8 March 1950

31

THE PEN IS MIGHTIER

A daily paper complains that there is too much snobbishness in the various enclosures at Epsom. And yet we distinctly saw one or two celebrities being allowed to mingle with the gossip-writers.

8 June 1932

At that moment his man came in with the new *Twaddler*, hot from the press.

I looked over Reginald's shoulder as he turned the pages with trembling hands.

There he was, alone, as he had said, and wearing the self-satisfied smirk which said plainly enough, 'Now you can withhold my rights no longer.' Plainly enough to me, that is: for the photographer had unfortunately failed to interpret it correctly, and below was the legend

'Evidently a backer of Braxted.'

Reginald flung down the paper and kicked a footstool savagely, and I decided it would be more tactful to leave him with his trouble.

At the door curiosity overcame discretion, however.

'*Did* you back Braxted?' I asked.

A copy of *The Turf Guide* struck the lintel a quarter of an inch above my head, and I closed the door hastily.

Evidently he had not.

BACKED TO WIN

At the conclusion of a steeplechase in America in which there were many spills it was found that three jockeys were on the wrong horses. And of course most of the general public as well.

12 April 1939

· FROM THE · HORSE'S MOUTH

OUR TURF PROPHETS.

[1929]

[An evening paper gave credit to the prophetic genius of its Racing Authority in the following terms: 'In his article on "The Best Outsider in the Derby" he wrote: "Trigo and Tom Peartree will appeal to those who dreamed that the winner's name started with a T."']

When on the Derby Stakes I bet
 (Out of respect for Institutions),
  I trust to others more expert
  To show me where to put my shirt,
People whose life-work is to get
 An inkling of the right solutions.

But nobody mentioned the winner before the race;
Nobody even fancied the brute for a place;
Merely we gathered the information (free)
That Trigo began with a T.

Sportsman. 'Wot won the big race? Let's 'ave a look, boy.'
Newsvendor (knowing the language). 'Some fancied Walloper; some were very sweet on Dolittle; Homing Pigeon had many friends. As they came into the straight it was anyone's race. The rest will cost you one penny, Sir.'

Nervous Punter (who has plunged on the favourite) 'There's
something about our bookie I don't like.'
Friend 'What—his face?'
Nervous Punter 'No, his running shoes.'

For weeks they'd studied every horse,
  Dodged in the dark their stable sentries,
    Marked their digestions, making notes
    About the way they took their oats,
  Wondered if they would stay the course,
    And felt the shins of all the entries.

But nobody mentioned the winner before the race,
  Even to say he had got a kindly face;
And this was their only hint for a mug like me,
    That Trigo began with a T.

You might suppose they're eating mud
  Because they overlooked his chances?
    Serenely they ignore their shame
    And keep on napping just the same,
  And still the thing they deemed a dud
    Will canter past their special fancies.

None of them mentioned the winner (at 33)
  Except to tell us his name began with a T;
But the bookies found, though nobody told them so,
    That it ends with a cheery O.

                                              O.S.

LATEST SPORTING
INTELLIGENCE
(*From our own Prophetic Correspondent*)
[1856]

Newmarket, Friday Evening

IT is now beyond doubt ascertained that *Spitfire* threw a shoe on Wednesday. I have just ascertained from Lewin, the Stable-boy, and who has been the winner in his day of nineteen cups and six saucers, a bit of the most important information. He assures me that *Ratcatcher* coughed and sneezed three times distinctly rather less than a month ago! This is genuine; for he was listening at the keyhole at the time and heard it himself. The affair soon got wind; and the consequence has been that the odds have gone down as much as two-sixteenths of a point. Baron Rothschild was at Tattersalls a few days since. He looked at *Polly* but didn't say a word. The greatest excitement prevails here respecting the Two Million Match on Wednesday next, between *Flatcatcher* and *The-Devil-among-the-Lawyers*. After much mental exertion, I venture to prophesy as follows, staking my reputation as usual upon the result:

Flatcatcher 1

The-Devil-among-the-Lawyers 2

Unless, by some extraordinary accident, the result should turn out to be:

The-Devil-among-the-Lawyers 1

Flatcatcher 2

Trainer. 'Now this horse is as fit as chemicals can make him. You've got a galvanic saddle, an electric whip, hypodermic spurs and if you can only shin a bit farther up his neck, you ought just to lick anything with hair on it.'

• A BIT OF •
A FLUTTER

THE LADIES' ART OF BETTING
[1848]

D0 NOT bet for money. It is vulgar, and was never meant to cross anything but a gipsey's hand. But gloves are open to you, and you are at liberty to bet as many pair as you like. You can do this very pleasantly over your chicken and champagne and the betting is not attended with any great risk, as you might foolishly imagine, for it stands to reason, that if you lose, you do not pay; and if you win, you are provided with gloves all the year round. Beware of defaulters, however; and do not bet with any gentleman who has not paid his last year's losses, or who is mean enough to remind you of your own.

Do not back the favourite, but take the entire field and by this means you have generally 10 good chances to 1 bad one. Always stipulate for French kid, if you win.

'When I think what I might have lost if it hadn't won I could
shoot myself for being such a fool as to back it.'

If your better is a very nice fellow, you can give him one of your gloves as a specimen, to treasure as a keepsake.

There is no Tattersall's for ladies where they can post their defaulters; it is usual to do it at the first quadrille or polka party they meet at after the Derby. Try requesting the address of his *gantier*; if he takes no notice of this hint then you are warranted in calling him a 'shabby fellow', or even a 'blackleg,' if you like, and in being always engaged 'six deep' when he asks you to dance.

Following the above rules of betting, a lady may find herself in gloves for every Horticultural, Floricultural, and Botanical fête during the season, at the very smallest cost.

'Excuse me, what won the three-thirty?'

A LULLABY

(For the Use of Sporting Nursemaids.)

[1901]

Baby darling, baby darling,
  Hushaby, no more be fretting.
Softly slumber while your nursie
    Gently reads to you the betting.
Baby darling, baby darling,
    Why so restless, why so cross?
Nurse will read you the 'arrivals,'
    And the latest from the course.

There, baby, there!
    Darling mustn't cry.
        If nurse's horse
        Can stay the course
    He'll pass the others by
And nurse will win, then baby shall
    Receive her little share
        Of nurse's bets,
        If gee-gee gets
    There, baby, there!

Baby darling, baby darling,
    Cease your weeping, there's a pet;
Do not sob because your nursie
    Has a little sporting bet.

43

Baby darling, baby darling,
  Do not purse your rose-bud lip
'Cos I'm going to have a shilling
  On a 'special stable tip.'

Hush, baby, hush!
  Darling mustn't cry.
    Nurse will show
    Baby how
  To flutter by-and-by.
And she shall have a bookie man
  Who lives in Shepherd's Bush
    And have a dash
    With dada's cash,
    Hush, baby, hush!

Baby darling, baby darling,
  Nursie is not always wrong.
Tho' she fancies dark outsiders
  At a price absurdly long.

Baby darling, baby darling,
  Do not always fear the worst;
One day nurse will back a gee-gee
  That will somehow get in first!

'Racing is like that, my dear. You win one day and you lose the next.'

'Why not come every other day, uncle?'

There, baby, there!
    Darling mustn't cry.
      Never mind,
      Nurse will find
    A winner by-and-by.
And we will risk a tiny sum
      Upon a likely mare
        And see her come
        A-romping home,
There! Baby, there!

A factory girl recently confessed that she had staked every penny she could borrow on a horse which afterwards won at 20 to 1. She was poor but she was on it.

6 September 1939

A HORSE ... A HORSE!
[1929]

A horse! a horse! I have a horse
Of great alacrity and force!
A lively eye within his head,
A neat industrious quadruped;
His food is kept inside a bin
And all his legs are rather thin;
Superb and resolute and swift,
I talk about him in the lift,
And all the typists say that he
Is quite a possibility.
The lift-man would not change a hair
Of him, nor the commissionaire.
The office-boy regards my horse
As suited to the Derby course;
His record in the past has not
Displeased the office-boy a lot
The office-boy would not repine
At owning such a horse as mine.

The colour of my horse is bay
(Or so the evening papers say),
And 'Spotlight' in his kindly way

47

:thelwell.

Has pointed out that no remorse
Will come from following my horse:
Magnificent, impetuous, kind,
My horse, it seems, is not inclined
To loaf about and feed on grass
While his contemporaries pass;
There may be other horses which
Lie down because they have a stitch,
Or jerk against the reins and sneeze,
But mine is not a horse like these.
There may be other horses who
Keep going zig-zag or askew,
But mine is not a horse like that,
He runs at a tremendous bat;
Sober, ingenious and good,
He acts precisely as he should
In simple unselfconsciousness
That captivates the morning Press.
I sometimes see his upper half
Depicted in a photograph,
And, though it only shows the bust,
He seems a horse that you can trust.
He had his home upon the crowns
Of one of our delightful downs,
The wind, the wheatears and the gorse

Are all familiar to my horse
He has observed the sea-mist rise
And listened to the curlew's cries
And heard the tinkling bell of sheep,
And I have got him fairly cheap
In fact, I drew him in a sweep

Owner. 'Why didn't you ride as I told you? Didn't I tell you to
force the pace early and come away at the Corner?'
Jockey. 'Yes, m'Lord, but I couldn't very well leave
the horse behind.'

He does not care about the tote
There is a shine upon his coat
The racing-colours he will bear
Are done in stripes like slumber-wear.
He does not understand divorce
My horse is a delightful horse
And everyone concurs with me
About his high velocity.

I often think of him at night
And wonder if he feels all right;
I should not like to have him brood
Or push away his cereal food.
My horse! with the impetuous crest,
So true to all that is the best
In England, and the unexpressed
Integrity of English lives!
They tell me he will start at fives
Or possibly at six to one
They tell me that my horse will run,
And if he does with self-control
With any luck he ought to roll
Up soonest at the winning-pole.

EVOE

51

· THE ·
SPECTATOR

from
A ROUGH GUIDE TO THE TURF
[1950]

THE question of *how* innumerable thousands of sports-men and women attain this corner of Suffolk on a weekday afternoon from such spots as Walthamstow, Sheffield, Birmingham and Westcliff-on-Sea – the coach inscriptions tell the tale – is, in my view, little more baffling than why. This genuinely puzzles me. In the 'Silver Ring' (admission ten shillings, no change given, no tickets issued, no re-admission, children must be paid for) it is possible, certainly, to see a 'brief, flashing fragment of each race: there is a concreted quadrangle running down to the rails, in which the bookmakers entice hoarsely and the tic-tac men follow their esoteric trade in white gloves, with holes in the thumbs, and from which the ruthless elbower may gain a position of vantage or, better still, at the back of the quadrangle is a tall flight of deep, concrete steps: from here, having fought for standing room with tooth and claw, though not an 'excuse me', unshaven sportsmen in mufflers and hay-headed youths in epauletted raincoats and saffron ties may see as much as a quarter of the one-mile course (though not, except with binoculars, the scoreboard).

Suppose six races to a meeting, and two minutes for each – the figures are rough: see Tuft and Dandelion for split-second statistics – then our sportsmen are going to see thirty seconds' racing in each race (provided other sportsmen don't shove their hats over their eyes), or a total of three minutes in the day's outing.

If you are the idle rich you can see the races like this –

and if you are the idle poor you get them this way.

It seems to me that one must do this thing in comfort, either on the spot but as a gentleman, with a comfortable seat, good binoculars, and a horse's-mouth winner, or at home with your feet on the mantelpiece and the evening paper in your hand; for Captain Tuft and Major Dandelion may be fallible as seers, but they give the results with honourable accuracy (if in rather small type sometimes), and in petrol, time, temper and plain nervous exhaustion the fireside sportsman will achieve a considerable saving.

J.B.B.

· DOWN ON · YOUR LUCK

THE BETTING-OFFICE FREQUENTER'S PROGRESS
[1852]

H<small>E WORE</small> a suit of Moses,
  The night when first we met,
And knowingly his hat was cocked
  Upon his curls of jet;
Flash 'Publics' he frequented,
  Where 'Sporting cards' were seen;
And many a Derby Sweep got up
  To ease them of their tin.
I saw him in his glory –
  (The word seems doubtful now),
When to his stable wisdom
  His admiring chums would bow.

A betting-book he'd started,
    When next this youth I saw;
And hourly he was lounging at
    Some Betting-Office door
Or standing treat to stable-boys
    With a 'weed' between his lips
And listening to their sage discourse
    Of 'great events' and ' tips'.
He told me then he stood to win
    A fi' pun' note or two,
Upon a 'certain' prophecy –
    I doubt if it came true.

And once again I see this youth,
    No betting-book is there:
The prison scissors close have cropped
    His once luxuriant hair.
They tell that 'cleaned' completely 'out,'
    He closed his short career
By bolting with his master's till,
    When 'settling' time drew near.
I see him shipped – the Government
    His passage out will pay:
And at some penal settlement,
    He'll spend his Settling Day.

THE TURF SPIDER AND THE FLIES

GEESE UPON THE TURF
[1867]

THE horse is a noble animal, and so, too, sometimes is its backer. But the equine nobility have this advantage over the human, – they have no family estates to put in jeopardy by racing. Whereas, in the past twelve-month, a good many noble sportsmen have travelled several downward stages on the road to ruin, through their gambling on the turf. In consequence a panic has ensued in the ring, and the betting men have pulled most dismally long faces at the short supply of cash. See here what sad news a turf writer reports:

> 'Complaints, and of an angry tone, were prevalent all last week in the turf market at the dreadful settling over the past Boughton meeting. Several noblemen and gentlemen who are the heaviest backers were unable to meet their liabilities and there was quite £70,000 short, which, of course, seriously depressed the financiers.'

Poor fellows! one is pained to hear of their distress. It is grievous to reflect that many a worthy bookmaker, instead of being able to afford himself champagne, as a wherewithal to raise his spirits from depression, may be reduced to gin-and-water, or plebeian half-and-half.

We rarely put much faith in any racing prophecy but we should rejoice greatly if this one were fulfilled. Every spring, however, sees a a fresh young flock of greenhorns going on the turf, where they are plucked as readily as geese upon a common: and after they have been parted with their fine old family timber, they usually find themselves completely up a tree.

We gather from an article on selective breeding it took two thousand years of selective breeding to produce the also-rans we backed last week.

8 March
1950

THE MAN AT THE BAR
[1933]

'IF you was Archbishop of Canterbury, I shouldn't
wonder,'
    Said the man at the bar,
If you was the Lord Chief Justice, and, by blooming thunder,
    I dessay you are
I tell you, it ain't any use for me to go racin',
    For as soon as I gets on a cert,
Flat racin' or hurdlin' or chasin',
    That 'orse is dirt.

'There's 'orses I've backed in my time as were taken with
    measles
    Right on the middle of the course
I'd safer put money on ferrets, I would, or on weasels
    Nor wot I would on a norse
There's jockeys turned round in a race and went back to
    the stable
    An' asked for a cup o' tea,
'Cos why? 'Cos they knew I was on 'em; and none wasn't
    able
    To ride against me.

There was horses were out-and-out naps from the very
    beginning,
    The papers they all said so,

'OAKS SURPRISE

'*Unknown Animal* wins in a canter' – *Daily Mail*

They said nothing on earth as was foaled could prevent 'em
from winning,
     But they didn't know.
There was 'orses could win in their sleep without waking
nor warning
     And roll past the judge on their head

They were scratched, 'cos the owner took ill on the very
    same morning
        And died in 'is bed,

I've followed their form, man and boy, for some forty-two
    seasons,
        An' I'll tell you one thing, my lad,
There's many a tipster will give you a dozen good reasons
        Why horses run bad
But there's only one reason which causes a reg'lar commotion
        To trainers and so on; ho yus!
'Alf Smith on that 'orse? ' say the bookies,'well, that's a fine
    notion!
        That's money for us.'

So whenever you bet on a race, and there's something you
	fancies,
		Over the sticks or the flat,
You ask what Alf Smith has a quid on afore taking chances,
		And don't bet on that
And I'd tell you the same – Here, Missy, another small
	brandy
		Said the man at the bar,
If you was the ex-King of Spain at this moment, or if you
	was Gandhi
		And I dessay you are!'

EVOE

Sportsman 'What on earth happened to the favourite?'
The Jonah 'I put money on him.'

EASY PROBLEM PICTURE: 'NAME THE WINNER!'